Remembering ROSALIND FRANKLIN

Rosalind Franklin & the Discovery of the Double Helix Structure of DNA

By **Tanya Lee Stone** • Illustrated by **Gretchen Ellen Powers**

Christy Ottaviano Books

LITTLE, BROWN AND COMPANY
New York   Boston

About This Book

The illustrations for this book were done in watercolor. This book was edited by Christy Ottaviano and designed by Megan McLaughlin. The production was supervised by Lillian Sun, and the production editor was Jen Graham. The text was set in Brandon Grotesque, and the display types are Just Lovely and Bon Vivant Serif.

Christy Ottaviano Books
Hachette Book Group
1290 Avenue of the Americas, New York, NY 10104
Visit us at LBYR.com

First Edition: February 2024

Christy Ottaviano Books is an imprint of Little, Brown and Company.
The Christy Ottaviano Books name and logo are trademarks of Hachette Book Group, Inc.

The publisher is not responsible for websites (or their content) that are not owned by the publisher.

Little, Brown and Company books may be purchased in bulk for business, educational, or promotional use. For information, please contact your local bookseller or the Hachette Book Group Special Markets Department at special.markets@hbgusa.com.

Library of Congress Cataloging-in-Publication Data
Names: Stone, Tanya Lee, author. | Powers, Gretchen Ellen, illustrator.
Title: Remembering Rosalind Franklin : Rosalind Franklin & the discovery of the double helix structure of DNA / written by Tanya Lee Stone ; illustrated by Gretchen Ellen Powers.
Description: First edition. | New York : Christy Ottaviano Books, Little, Brown and Company, 2024. | Includes bibliographical references. | Audience: Ages 5–9 | Summary: "An inspiring nonfiction picture book about Rosalind Franklin, the groundbreaking chemist who helped discover the structure of DNA, by the award-winning, bestselling author of Who Says Women Can't Be Doctors? and Elizabeth Leads the Way." —Provided by publisher.
Identifiers: LCCN 2022052198 | ISBN 9780316351249 (hardcover)
Subjects: LCSH: Franklin, Rosalind, 1920-1958—Juvenile literature. | Women molecular biologists—Great Britain—Biography—Juvenile literature. | Molecular biologists—Great Britain—Biography—Juvenile literature. | DNA—History—Juvenile literature.
Classification: LCC QH506 .S825 2024 | DDC 572.8092 [B]—dc23/eng/20230126
LC record available at https://lccn.loc.gov/2022052198

ISBN 978-0-316-35124-9

PRINTED IN CHINA

APS

10 9 8 7 6 5 4 3 2 1

For anyone who did something awesome and didn't feel the love.

And for Jake and Liza, always.

—TLS

For Momma, Da, and my brother, Seth—my loves, my life, my blood . . .

my lifeblood. There's no one else on earth I'd rather share DNA with.

—GEP

Dear Reader,

This true story doesn't really have a happy ending.

Why would I start by telling you that? Because sometimes a person can do something extraordinary and *not* get the win. They don't become famous, or earn a prize, or live happily ever after. Sometimes, they never even find out they made a difference.

Often when we hear about something that's never been done before, it's about the people who got there first—to land on the moon, cure a disease, or unlock a mystery. But nobody achieves such great things alone. There are usually other people whose hard work made change possible. Stories about those people are just as important. And it's up to us to remember them.

This story is about remembering Rosalind.

Rosalind Elsie Franklin was born in 1920 and was the second-oldest child in a big, bustling Jewish family in London, England. They were a talkative lot, outspoken and honest, arguing good-naturedly about all manner of things.

Rosalind and her siblings enjoyed beach holidays together and visiting their grandparents' country house—rolling down hills and chasing chickens. Rosalind was especially fascinated with the darkroom, swirling crystal chemicals in a tub with special paper, making photographic images come to life.

At this time, it wasn't common for girls to think about college and careers. But Rosalind's parents expected just as much from their daughters as their sons. Although she stressed about homework and exams, Rosalind threw herself into everything she did, equally excelling at tennis and hockey as geography and German.

While she loved solving puzzles and problems, Rosalind did not have a knack for music. One cannot be good at *everything*.

She found math and science quite exciting, and by age fifteen, chemistry and physics were particular passions. That same year, Rosalind's parents took her to Norway, sparking her lifelong love for climbing mountains.

Within a few years, Rosalind was ready to get on with becoming a scientist. Even though there were very few women in science, this didn't stop her. She set her sights on the University of Cambridge and scored higher than anyone else who took the chemistry test.

Rosalind dove into her studies and joined a math society. After graduating and doing an extra year of research, she looked for work. There was a war going on, and Rosalind wanted to use her skills to help.

Gas masks kept people from breathing in dangerous chemicals from bombs. The filters in the masks used coal to absorb the chemicals, but some types of coal worked better than others. Rosalind's job was to figure out why. Her work made gas masks safer by showing how different kinds of coal behaved at different temperatures and pressures.

Rosalind had a zest for life. Even her idea of relaxing was vigorous. Cooking turned into hosting dinner parties. Going for a bike ride could mean a fifty-mile jaunt. And to climb a high peak with a friend was her idea of heaven.

In the summer of 1946, Rosalind went to France to climb the Alps. "I could wander happily in France for ever," she wrote. Lucky for her, she was soon offered a research job in Paris. Having spent time just outside Paris before college, Rosalind spoke excellent French.

At the French lab, Rosalind continued studying coals and carbons. She became an expert at X-ray crystallography, using X-rays to look at atoms and molecules tens of thousands of times smaller than anything the human eye can see. With this technique, she could discover the invisible structure inside tiny specks of matter, which became to her "as real and solid as billiard balls."

An X-ray crystallographer shoots invisible X-rays through a crystal that bounce off the crystal's atoms, or diffract, and create a pattern on a photographic plate. At the time, scientists had to measure each spot in the diffraction pattern by hand and use math to figure out how the atoms fit together in three dimensions. The material had to be prepared and positioned just right. Rosalind was so talented at this that one of her fellow scientists remarked on her "golden hands."

Women scientists were not as rare in France as they were in England. They were also treated with more respect and paid the same as men. Rosalind's fast and animated way of talking was admired; her colleagues found her quite smart. The fashion there was also smart, and Rosalind was enthralled. One day, she visited a laboratory sporting the newest look from famous designer Christian Dior!

Although she loved living and working in Paris, and having travel adventures with her friends, Rosalind missed her family. There was also trailblazing work happening back in London. Scientists were using X-ray crystallography in biological substances instead of only minerals like carbon. When a position came up at King's College, Rosalind took it and started studying DNA.

DNA stands for *deoxyribonucleic acid*. It is the genetic code inside every cell of every living thing. It's what makes you—YOU. And DNA holds the instructions for any organism to grow, survive, and reproduce—whether it's a plant, a puppy, a platypus, or every person on the planet!

Back then, scientists weren't convinced that DNA carried the genetic code, and it wasn't understood how hereditary information was passed from parents to children—in other words, why you might look very much like one of your parents. Scientists needed to learn more about DNA's structure.

James Watson and Francis Crick were studying DNA at nearby University of Cambridge. Linus Pauling was doing the same in California. Rosalind was suddenly part of an unofficial race to figure out what would become known as the secret of life.

19

Rosalind understood that she had been hired to direct the X-ray diffraction work on DNA. She was given an assistant—Raymond Gosling—who was talented, hardworking, and cheerful. Maurice Wilkins had been the lead DNA scientist at King's College, and he was under the impression Rosalind was hired to be *his* assistant. Rosalind and Maurice got off on the wrong foot and stayed there, never sorting out the misunderstanding.

While King's College did not feel friendly to her, Rosalind did not want to waste time dealing with personality problems. She had better things to do.

With her camera, she got to it. Soon, her X-ray diffraction images revealed incredible results. Rosalind discovered that DNA created different patterns depending on whether it was wet or dry.

All the images scientists had taken up until then had blurred the two forms together, making the photographs difficult to interpret. When Rosalind presented her discovery at a lecture, James Watson was in the audience.

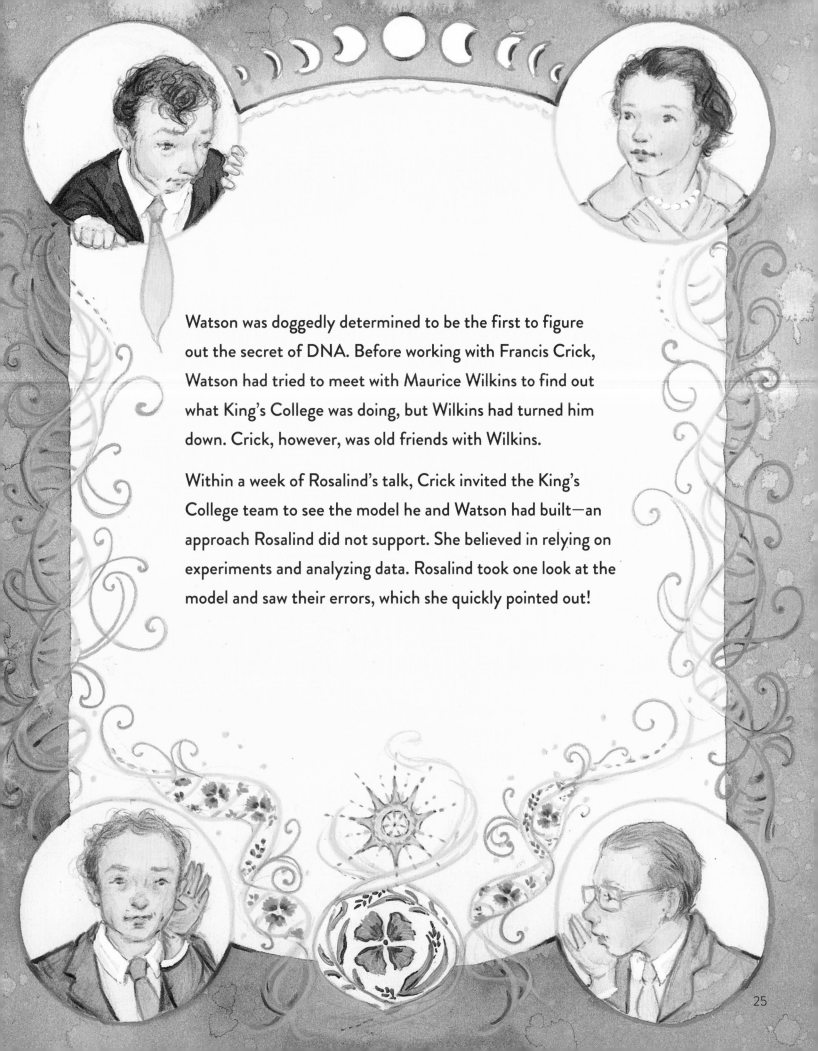

Watson was doggedly determined to be the first to figure out the secret of DNA. Before working with Francis Crick, Watson had tried to meet with Maurice Wilkins to find out what King's College was doing, but Wilkins had turned him down. Crick, however, was old friends with Wilkins.

Within a week of Rosalind's talk, Crick invited the King's College team to see the model he and Watson had built—an approach Rosalind did not support. She believed in relying on experiments and analyzing data. Rosalind took one look at the model and saw their errors, which she quickly pointed out!

Back in her lab, Rosalind kept creating beautiful X-ray diffraction images. But the best was yet to come.

In May 1952, she set up her camera.

The image she captured was superb. And it contained an enormous amount of information that would become the key to understanding the structure of DNA.

She labeled it simply . . .

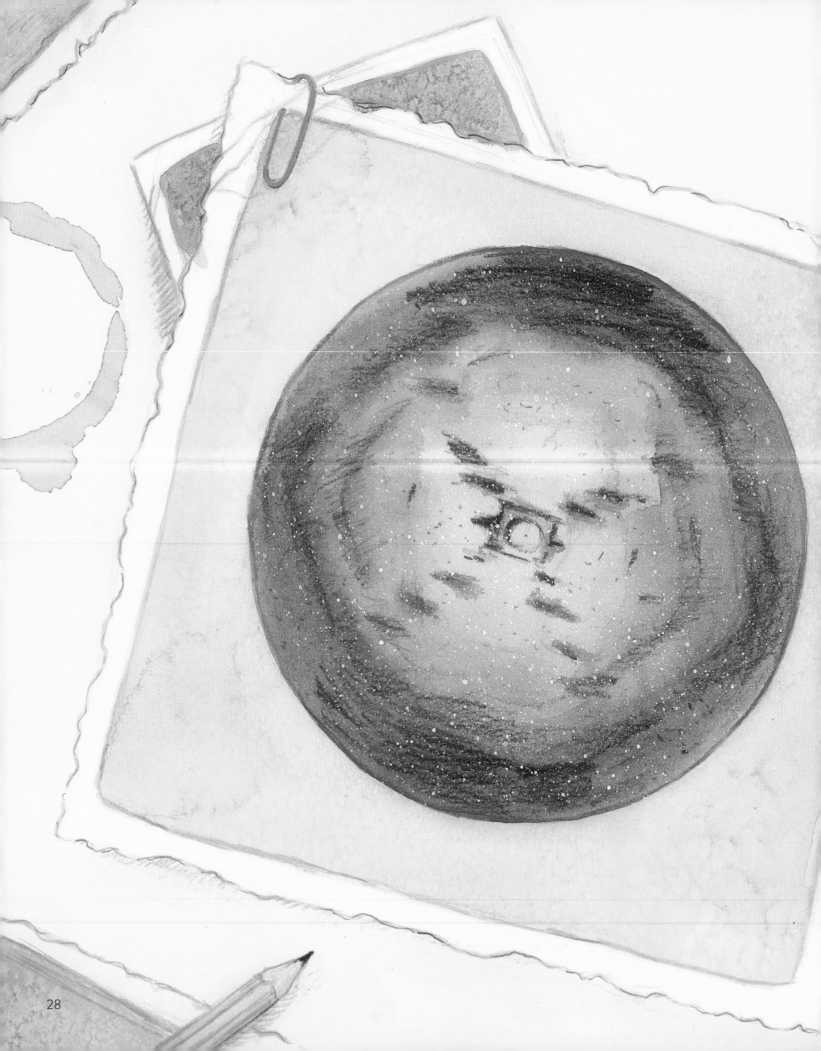

...PHOTO 51.

But despite her desire to solve this mystery, Rosalind could no longer stand how unfriendly the environment felt at King's College. As a woman, she wasn't even welcome in the senior common room, where many of the staff ate lunch.

Soon, Rosalind lined up another job. She would throw herself into a new project just as she had done earlier. Before leaving, she wrote up everything she had discovered as part of her lab's end-of-the-year progress report.

Now here's where the story takes a turn for the worse.

31

There are many different accounts about how Maurice Wilkins ended up with Rosalind's *Photo 51*. But what we do know is that Wilkins showed it to Watson and that Rosalind was never consulted.

"The instant I saw the picture my mouth fell open and my pulse began to race," Watson later wrote. The X pattern clearly indicated DNA had the shape of a helix, or spiral.

Watson and Crick then got hold of the end-of-the-year report. There, in Rosalind's section, was her description of a single building block of DNA, along with her carefully calculated measurements.

Rosalind's data told Crick that DNA must be a *pair* of spirals—one running up, the other down, creating a double helix. The double helix structure would allow DNA to split down the middle and make copies of itself. Within weeks, Watson and Crick completed a correct model of DNA, fully cracking the code to the secret of life.

And so, dear reader, as I warned, this true story does not have a particularly happy ending. Rosalind never learned that Watson and Crick couldn't have done it without her *Photo 51*. She died in 1958, four years before Watson and Crick won the Nobel Prize, along with Wilkins, for their discovery of the double helix.

So how do *we* know the story? In a twist of fate, in 1968, it was Watson himself who piqued people's interest, after writing a book about discovering the structure of DNA. In it, he talked about Rosalind. Imagine a scientist writing about one of his colleagues this way:

"Clearly Rosy [a nickname she did not like] had to go or be put in her place."

And "there was no denying she had a good brain. If she could only keep her emotions under control, there would be a good chance that she could really help."

And "she was not unattractive and might have been quite stunning had she taken even a mild interest in clothes." (Of course, you've already learned that she liked fashion, so this comment is not only obnoxious, it's untrue!)

Watson's words were noticed. People started looking into her story. And they learned all about Rosalind's real role.

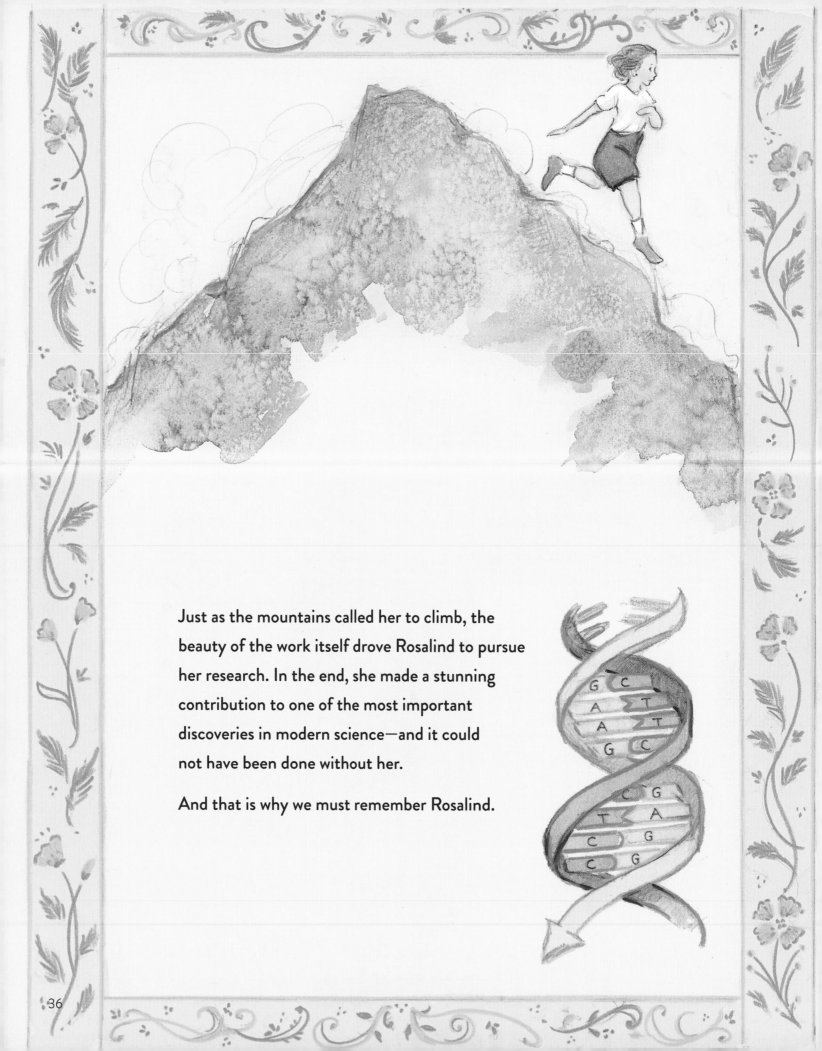

Just as the mountains called her to climb, the beauty of the work itself drove Rosalind to pursue her research. In the end, she made a stunning contribution to one of the most important discoveries in modern science—and it could not have been done without her.

And that is why we must remember Rosalind.

Author's Note
A BIT MORE, PLUS THE MATILDA EFFECT

Rosalind Franklin was born on July 25, 1920, in the Notting Hill neighborhood of London, England. From the time she was tiny, she had an impressive presence. Bright and independent, she embraced life and excelled at most things she tried. She was close to her siblings, spoke up for what she believed in (sometimes even arguing with her imposing father), and had big dreams and strived for them. I was instantly drawn to her story—but it took a long time for me to even know she *had* a story.

One of my favorite types of stories to tell are about real women who have done extraordinary things to help shape our world. Too often, these true stories are not in our history books. Even worse, for hundreds of years, countless women's achievements haven't just been overlooked—the credit for their work has been claimed by men. This is now called the Matilda Effect, named after Matilda Joslyn Gage, who spoke about this pattern of injustice in the late 1800s. Gage was one of the original founders of the National Woman Suffrage Association in 1869 (founded to fight for women's right to vote) alongside heroes Susan B. Anthony and Elizabeth Cady Stanton. Gage helped Anthony and Stanton write the Declaration of Rights and Sentiments, challenging the fact that women were not included in the Declaration of Independence, which only stated that "all men are created equal."

Rosalind Franklin at the microscope.

Just as it has taken centuries for society to start treating women equally (women didn't even win the right to vote in America until 1920), women's histories have not been given equal weight. I was in my twenties, earning a master's degree in science, when I first learned about a woman named Rosalind Franklin—directly from Francis Crick himself! My father, a science professor, had invited him to guest lecture at his university, and Crick was staying at our family home. One evening, at the dinner table, Crick talked about Rosalind Franklin. He spoke kindly of her, the work she did on the structure of DNA, and his regrets about how she was treated. I was surprised not to recognize her name, given the fact that the double helix structure of DNA is one of the most important scientific discoveries of all time. I had only ever been taught that Francis Crick and James Watson were responsible for this monumental achievement.

Rosalind Franklin on a family holiday in Norway.

As you have read in this book, Rosalind Franklin is at the heart of this scientific story. It was her *Photo 51* that provided the missing piece of the DNA puzzle, showing the double helix structure. Her work was what allowed Watson and Crick to fully understand all the research that had been conducted up to that point and create an accurate model of the structure of DNA. And, as you have also read here, Franklin did not know they obtained her photo and never became aware that it was her work that ultimately unlocked the mystery.

Tragically, Rosalind Franklin died at the young age of thirty-seven from ovarian cancer. But in her brief career, she helped change what we know about DNA. Although she was not able to personally enjoy recognition for those achievements during her lifetime, Franklin's story and her accomplishments are now understood. My hope is that young readers will learn her name and dig more deeply into her scientific work, further honoring and remembering Rosalind for her invaluable contributions to science.

Quotes

Page 12   "I could wander happily in France for ever." Maddox, *Rosalind Franklin*, 84.

Page 14   "as real and solid as billiard balls." Maddox, *Rosalind Franklin*, 56.

Page 15   "golden hands." Maddox, *Rosalind Franklin*, 95.

Page 33   "The instant I saw the picture my mouth fell open and my pulse began to race." Watson, *The Double Helix*, 181.

Page 35   "Clearly Rosy had to go or be put in her place." Watson, *The Double Helix*, 12.

Page 35   "There was no denying she had a good brain. If she could only keep her emotions under control, there would be a good chance that she could really help." Watson, *The Double Helix*, 12.

Page 35   "she was not unattractive and might have been quite stunning had she taken even a mild interest in clothes." Watson, *The Double Helix*, 10.

Sources

Carina, Dennis, and Richard Gallagher, eds. *The Human Genome*. New York: Nature Publishing Group, 2001.

Crick, Francis. *What Mad Pursuit: A Personal View of Scientific Discovery*. New York: HarperCollins, 1988.

Glassman, Gary, dir. "Secret of Photo 51." *NOVA*. Boston: WBGH, 2003.

Glynn, Jenifer. *My Sister Rosalind Franklin*. Oxford, England: Oxford University Press, 2012.

Grady, Denise. "A Revolution at 50: 50 Years Later, Rosalind Franklin's X-Ray Fuels Debate." *New York Times*, February 25, 2003.

Maddox, Brenda. *Rosalind Franklin: The Dark Lady of DNA*. New York: HarperCollins, 2002.

Sayre, Anne. *Rosalind Franklin and DNA*. New York: W. W. Norton, 1975.

Watson, James D. *The Double Helix: A Personal Account of the Discovery of the Structure of DNA*. New York: Atheneum, 1968.